AGB SPECIAL REPORT

S0-DPP-479

Composition of Governing Boards, 1985

A Survey of College and University Boards

Prepared by the Association of Governing Boards

In cooperation with the Higher Education Panel of the

American Council on Education

Made possible by a grant from Chemical Bank

Contents

301583

Foreword

*T*he *Composition of Governing Boards, 1985* is an update of the 1977
survey, *Composition of College and University Governing Boards,*
conducted for the Association of Governing Boards by the Higher Education Panel of the American Council on Education. The original survey
offered some general insight into the makeup of college and university boards
and the various characteristics of the people who served on them.

This 1985 update includes many of the same questions asked in 1977 but
has been expanded to allow for greater understanding of such characteristics
as the professional background of board members, the types and number of
other boards (both profit and not-for-profit) on which these people serve; con-
stituent representation; and so on. These and other characteristics are high-
lighted in the first section of the report; for comparison, the highlights from
the 1977 survey can be found in Appendix C.

The data for the 1985 survey were gathered and analyzed by the Higher
Education Panel of the American Council on Education. A total of 215 single-
campus boards and 157 multicampus boards provided the information that
was then statistically adjusted to represent the traits of the 2,200 boards
governing the nation's 3,000 nonprofit institutions of higher education.

The growth in corporate involvement in this voluntary service is a posi-
tive one. Attracting participation from those beyond corporate chairs and CEOs
is a credit to the higher education institutions and to corporate support for
community voluntary involvement.

But more needs to be done—particularly with women and minorities on
college and university boards. Board composition and the selection process
ultimately determine college and university policy making. We must do the
best we can to choose the best people possible to govern higher education.

Charles J. Andersen directed the study and wrote the report. Special
thanks goes to Nancy Suniewick for her efforts in the early stages of the survey
draft and to the late Frank J. Atelsek, former director of the Higher Education
Panel. Richard D. Legon and Linda E. Henderson of AGB coordinated the plan-
ning and managed the production of the survey.

We are indebted to the Chemical Bank, to its president, Robert Callander,
and to his colleagues, for the generous support of and interest in the study.
Special thanks also goes to William G. Wehner, vice president for development
and university relations at Drew University, for his assistance in securing the
funds to make this project possible.

Robert L. Gale
President
Association of Governing Boards
of Universities and Colleges

Methods Summary

*T*he *Composition of Governing Boards, 1985* survey form (see Appendix B) was mailed in April 1985 to two classes of Higher Education Panel (HEP) institutions: (1) single-campus institutions, those whose boards are responsible for only one campus each; and (2) multicampus institutions, those whose boards are legally responsible for the control of two or more campuses or institutions. In addition, questionnaires were sent to multicampus institutions whose members are not part of HEP. These institutions were identified using various information sources including the Association of Governing Boards of Universities and Colleges (AGB). Therefore, estimates for the single-campus institutions are based on a sample, and figures for the multicampus boards come from a survey of the total population of such boards.

Nonrespondents were followed up by mail and telephone contacts. By the close of the field phase in August, usable data had been obtained from 75 percent of the single-campus boards and 85 percent of the multicampus boards queried.

The estimates reported in this publication were developed first by classifying institutions into relatively homogeneous strata and then applying weights to questionnaire item responses. The single-campus boards were stratified according to the standard HEP stratification plan which is based on the type, control, and size of an institution. The multicampus boards were stratified according to their control and type. Responses to each item were then weighted within each stratification cell by the ratio of the number of boards in the population to the number of responding boards in the cell. The weighted responses were aggregated into broad categories appropriate to the survey analysis.

Highlights

Board Profile

- An estimated 48,000 trustees and regents serve on 2,200 governing boards responsible for 3,000 colleges and universities. Approximately 86 percent of these board members (41,500) are in the independent sector of higher education.

- Multicampus boards (approximately 200 in all) make up less than 10 percent of the total but govern one-third of all campuses, representing just over half (55 percent) of the nation's student population. Most multicampus boards are public.

- Boards governing independent institutions average 28 active voting trustees; boards governing public institutions average 9 trustees.

Trustee Profile

- Twenty percent of all board members (9,600) are women (up from 15 percent in 1977).

- Six percent of board members (3,000) are black—a percentage that has not changed since 1977.

- Ninety-three percent of all trustees have at least a baccalaureate, and 30 percent have a professional or doctoral degree.

- Approximately one-third of all board members are between the ages of 50 and 59; one-third are under 50; and one-third are 60 or older.

- Thirty-seven percent of all board members are business executives (plus another four percent who are retired from business careers, for a total of 41 percent) as compared to 34 percent in 1977.

- Eighteen percent of all trustees are presidents of corporations or board chairpersons; 27 percent of all trustees are members of at least one corporate board.

- Ten percent of trustees (4,800) serve on more than one governing board.

- Twenty-eight percent of all board members are alumni of the institutions they serve.

Governing Boards: How Many and What Kind

*M*ore than 2,200 boards of trustees govern the nation's 3,000 nonprofit institutions of postsecondary education that, in turn, enroll more than 8-million full-time-equivalent (FTE) students. A board might control only one campus with 100 students or a board might govern as many as 64 campuses enrolling 380,000 students.

Less than 10 percent (or 187) of all boards are multicampus; that is, they control more than one campus. Such boards are responsible for just under 1,000 individual campuses that, in 1984, had an enrollment of more than 4.5-million FTE students—over half of the national total.

(The remaining 2,000 boards govern individual campuses that enroll just under 4-million FTE students.)

Most (82 percent) of the multicampus boards are public; they govern 90 percent of the campuses in multicampus systems. The public multicampus institutions vary widely in size—from 2 to 64 campuses. None of the *independent* multicampus boards govern more than four campuses.

(This survey included only not-for-profit institutions. Consequently, excluded were the approximately 200 proprietary business and technical schools that have campuses in various cities, nationwide.)

The Characteristics of Board Members

Board Members: How Many Are There?

*T*he nation's 2,200 governing boards have nearly 52,000 authorized voting member positions. This figure is exclusive of honorary or emeritus positions that might exist but were not examined by this survey. It is also exclusive of any non-voting faculty or student positions.

The number of individuals who are actually *serving* on our nation's governing boards is less than the 52,000 figure, because almost 4,000 authorized positions remain unfilled at any given time. Furthermore, institutions report that about ten percent of the board members serve on more than one college or university board.

The 48,000 active positions on college and university governing boards are filled by men and women with varied racial/ethnic, educational, and occupational backgrounds. A small fraction of them—only about five percent—serve on multicampus boards. The remainder are on boards responsible for a single campus.

Most of the board members (86 percent) serve on boards of independent institutions. Three reasons explain this: (1) independent boards, on the average, have more board members than do public ones; (2) there are more independent than public boards; and (3) multicampus systems are more prevalent in the public sector. This distribution is almost the reverse of the distribution of *students* between the public and independent sectors: Eighty percent of the students in higher education are enrolled in public institutions; 20 percent are in independent colleges and universities.

Figures A and B contrast the number and the average size of public and independent boards.

Board Members: Who Are They?

Occupation

Five categories were identified to provide a framework for grouping board members by occupation: (1) business, (2) education, (3) professional services, (4) retired status, and (5) "other" occupations.

Business. Thirty-seven percent or 18,000 of all board members are from business. A little more than one-third of these individuals are executives of large business corporations, 25 percent are from banking, financial, insurance, or real estate companies, and the remaining (37 percent) are executives of small businesses, entrepreneurs, or owners of their own businesses.

FIGURE A
Number of Governing Boards
by Type of Board and Control of Institution

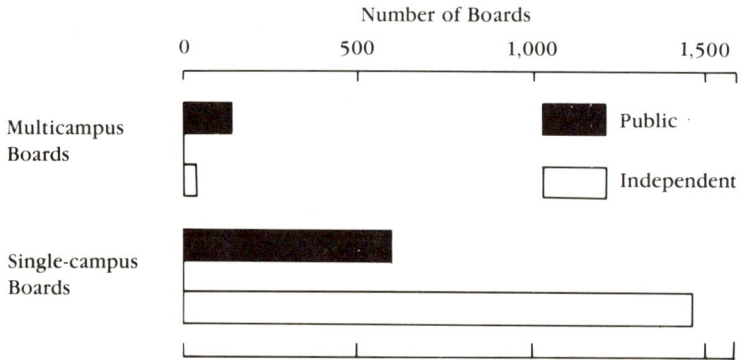

Number of Boards

| 0 | 500 | 1,000 | 1,500 |

Multicampus
Boards

■ Public

□ Independent

Single-campus
Boards

FIGURE B
Average Size of Governing Board by Type
of Board and Control of Institution

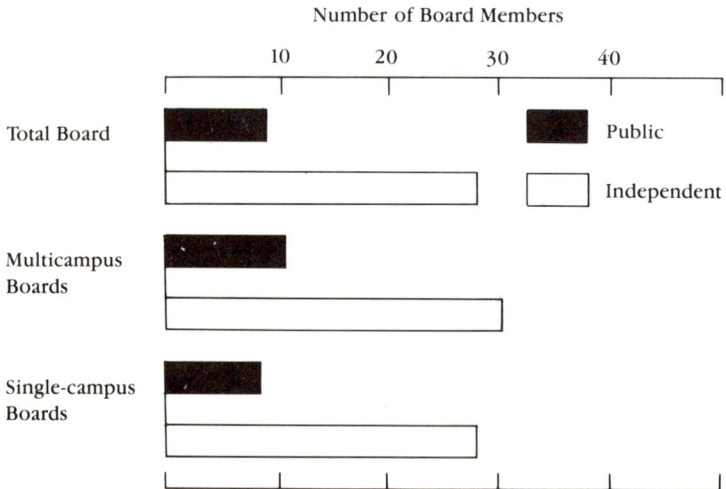

Number of Board Members

| 10 | 20 | 30 | 40 |

Total Board

■ Public

□ Independent

Multicampus
Boards

Single-campus
Boards

(The terms "large business corporations" and "smaller business" were not specifically defined in the original questionnaire. Neither were guidelines given to distinguish a "large business corporation" from the "banking, financial, insurance, or real estate company." The proportions shown should therefore be considered as indications of general magnitudes or relationships, not as precise percentages.)

Four percent of the board members are retired from business occupations. Addition of these former members of the business community to those on the active roster brings to 41 percent the proportion of board members who are or have been in business.

Just over 25 percent of the college and university board members also sit on corporate boards providing still another link between higher education and the business community.

Eighteen percent of college and university board members are the chairperson, chief executive officer, or chief operating officer of a corporation. Relating this figure to the primary occupation data indicates that nearly half of the business representatives on institutional governing boards come from the top levels of management.

Education. Eleven percent of the board members are in the field of education. Seven percent are administrators, faculty, or students in institutions of higher education. Four percent are teachers or administrators in elementary or secondary schools or systems.

Professional Services. The primary occupation of 14 percent of all board members is reported as being in one of the professions (other than education or religion). Figure C shows those professions that were specifically identified. Law (seven percent of the total) is the profession most heavily represented.

Retired Persons. Figure C also shows that 10 percent of board members are drawn from the ranks of retirees. Almost half of these individuals have been corporate or financial officers; about 20 percent have had careers in education.

Other Occupations. This general category accounts for 28 percent of all board members. By far, the largest proportion of this subgroup is members of the clergy; they account for 13 percent of all board members and therefore almost half of the "other" occupational category. Table 4 (see Appendix A) shows that their representation is minimal (only one percent) on public boards, but significant in the independent sector (15 percent of single-campus boards and six percent of multicampus boards).

Homemakers represent five percent of all board members and are more frequently found at single-campus institutions than at multicampus institutions. Just the reverse is true for government officials, both elected and nonelected. They represent two percent of the total single-campus institutions, but about four percent on multicampus boards (see Table 4).

Selected Demographics.
Sex. Eighty percent of all board members are men. Boards of public institutions have a higher percentage of women than do those in the independent sector. In none of the major institutional classifications, however, do women represent more than 25 percent of the total.

Race/ethnicity. The vast majority of board members—approximately 90 percent—are white. Six percent are black and less than one percent are Hispanic. The estimated number of other racial/ethnic groups' (Asian, Native American) members is three percent of the total.

FIGURE C
Primary Occupation of Board Members

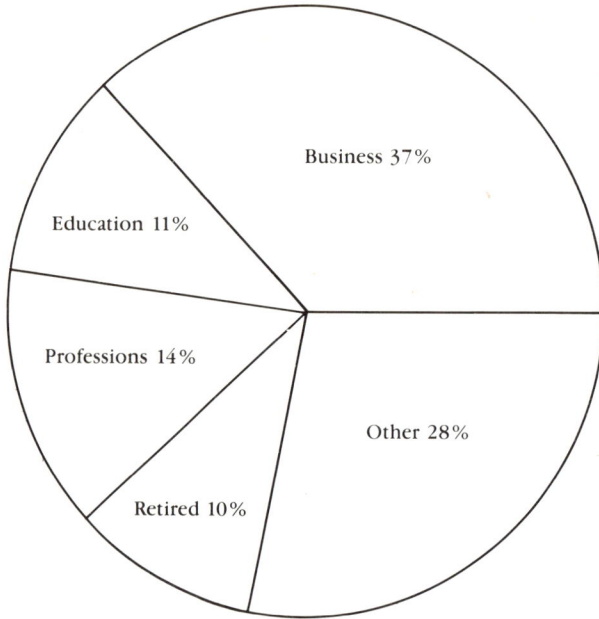

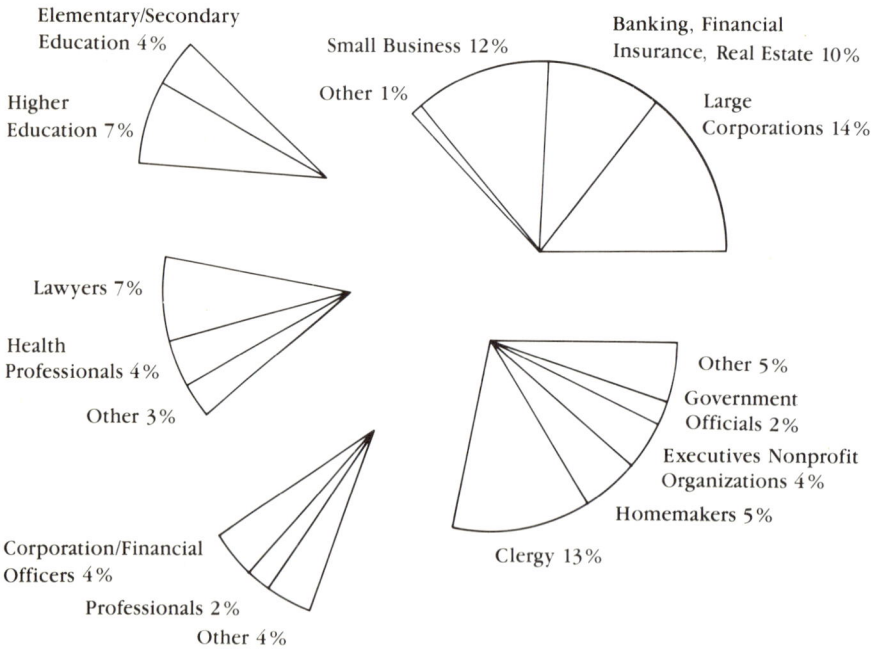

Business 37%

Education 11%

Professions 14%

Retired 10%

Other 28%

Elementary/Secondary Education 4%

Higher Education 7%

Small Business 12%

Other 1%

Banking, Financial Insurance, Real Estate 10%

Large Corporations 14%

Lawyers 7%

Health Professionals 4%

Other 3%

Other 5%

Government Officials 2%

Executives Nonprofit Organizations 4%

Homemakers 5%

Clergy 13%

Corporation/Financial Officers 4%

Professionals 2%

Other 4%

Educational Attainment. More than 90 percent of board members have at least a bachelor's degree. Eleven percent of board members have a doctorate and 19 percent reported they have professional degrees as their highest educational credential. Independent institutions report a higher percentage of board members with doctoral degrees than do public institutions. Public institutions, however, have a higher percentage of board members with professional degrees (see Figure D).

Age. The age range with more governing board members than any other is 50 to 59 years. More than one-third of the members fall into that span. About 25 percent are in the next older age range (60 to 69 years) and 20 percent are in the next younger (40 to 49 years).

Approximately 75 percent of the members on independent boards are 50 years or older, compared to 60 percent at public institutions. At the other end of the age scale, just over two percent of the independent board members are 30 years old or younger; a little less than two percent of public board members are in that age range.

Special Requirements

Some institutions require that a specific number or proportion of board members come from special constituencies. Two specific constituencies—sponsoring church organization and alumni status—were identified on the survey questionnaire. Additionally, an "other special constituency" option was included.

Eleven thousand board positions, about 25 percent of the total, are held by individuals who must come from the institutions' sponsoring church organizations. These individuals are on boards exclusively in the private sector.

A much smaller number of board seats—about 2,500—are required to be held by alumni of the institution. This requirement is found in all types of institutions—public and independent, multi and single-campus. At independent multicampus institutions, 12 percent of the board positions have to be filled by alumni. This contrasts with public single-campus colleges where the comparable proportion is less than one percent.

About 6,500 other board seats have to be filled by individuals from some other special constituency. In many cases this requirement is found at public institutions and is related to political office or residence, e.g., the governor of the state, a state legislator, or residence in the community college district.

Representation from the institution itself can take the form not only of those alumni who are *required* to be on the board, but of faculty, students, and additional alumni who have been selected for membership. Faculty and student members account for less than three percent of the total. Total alumni—required and additional—come to 28 percent of all board members. Independent institutions include more alumni proportionally than do public institutions (see Figure E). (It should be remembered that these data relate to *voting* governing board members actually serving on the board. There are many institutions that have nonvoting student or faculty education, but such individuals are *not* included in these estimates.)

FIGURE D
Highest Level of Education Attained by Governing Board Members

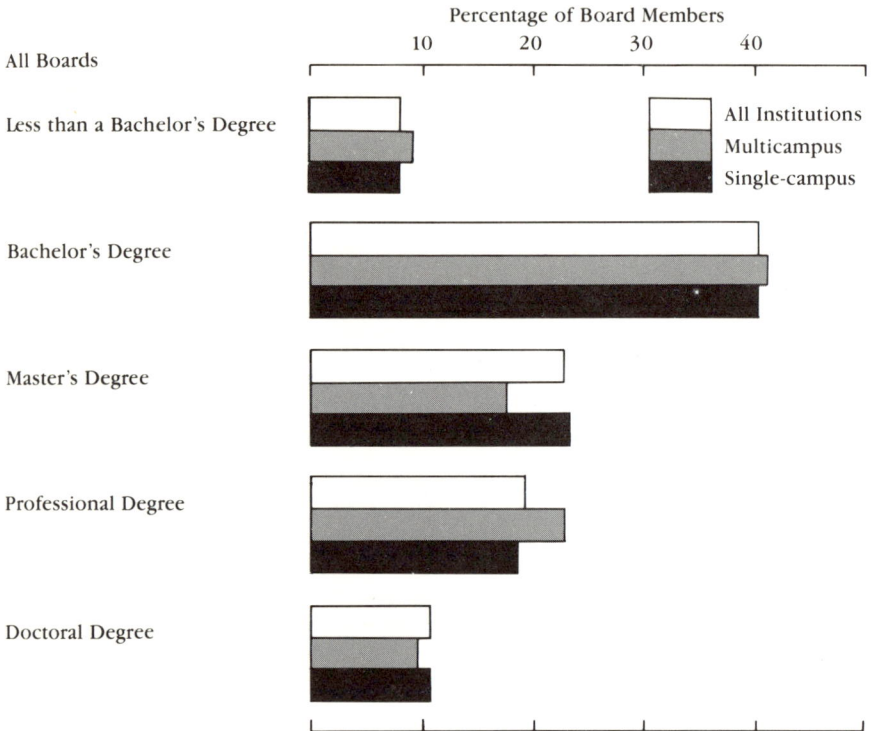

Percentage of Board Members

All Boards

Less than a Bachelor's Degree

☐ All Institutions
▨ Multicampus
■ Single-campus

Bachelor's Degree

Master's Degree

Professional Degree

Doctoral Degree

FIGURE E
Percent of Board Members Who are Alumni of the Institutions They Serve

	Total Alumni Serving	Total Alumni Required	Additional Alumni Serving
All Institutions	28.2	5.1	23.1
Public	13.0	1.6	11.4
Independent	31.0	6.0	25.0

Contrasts Between Multicampus and Single-Campus Boards

*I*t was noted earlier that 187 multicampus boards had been identified for the purposes of this study. They govern nearly 1,000 individual campuses that enroll more than 4.5 million full-time-equivalent students. The overwhelming majority of these boards are in the public sector (154 or 82 percent); they govern 914 (92 percent) of the individual campuses for an average of 5.9 campuses per board. In contrast, the 33 independent multicampus boards govern only 75 campuses for an average of just under 2.3 campuses per board.

The average size of the public multicampus board is only about one-third the size of the comparable board in the private sector—10 members in contrast to over 30. This means that although 80 percent of the multicampus *boards* are public, only 60 percent of all board *members* serving on them are from the public sector.

Public single-campus boards are also smaller than independent single-campus boards. The former average about eight members per board; the latter nearly 30 members.

One-third of all multicampus boards have at least one large public research university. Another third of the multicampus boards govern public two-year colleges.

Figure F contrasts multicampus and single-campus boards on a number of characteristics. In general, multicampus boards have a higher percentage of members in business and the professions than do single-campus boards.

The proportion of board members who are *required* to be graduates of the governed institution is higher for the multicampus institutions than for single-campus ones. And the total share of alumni board members is also higher among the multicampus boards than at the single-campuses—34 percent to 28 percent.

FIGURE F
Selected Characteristics of Board Members by Type of Board

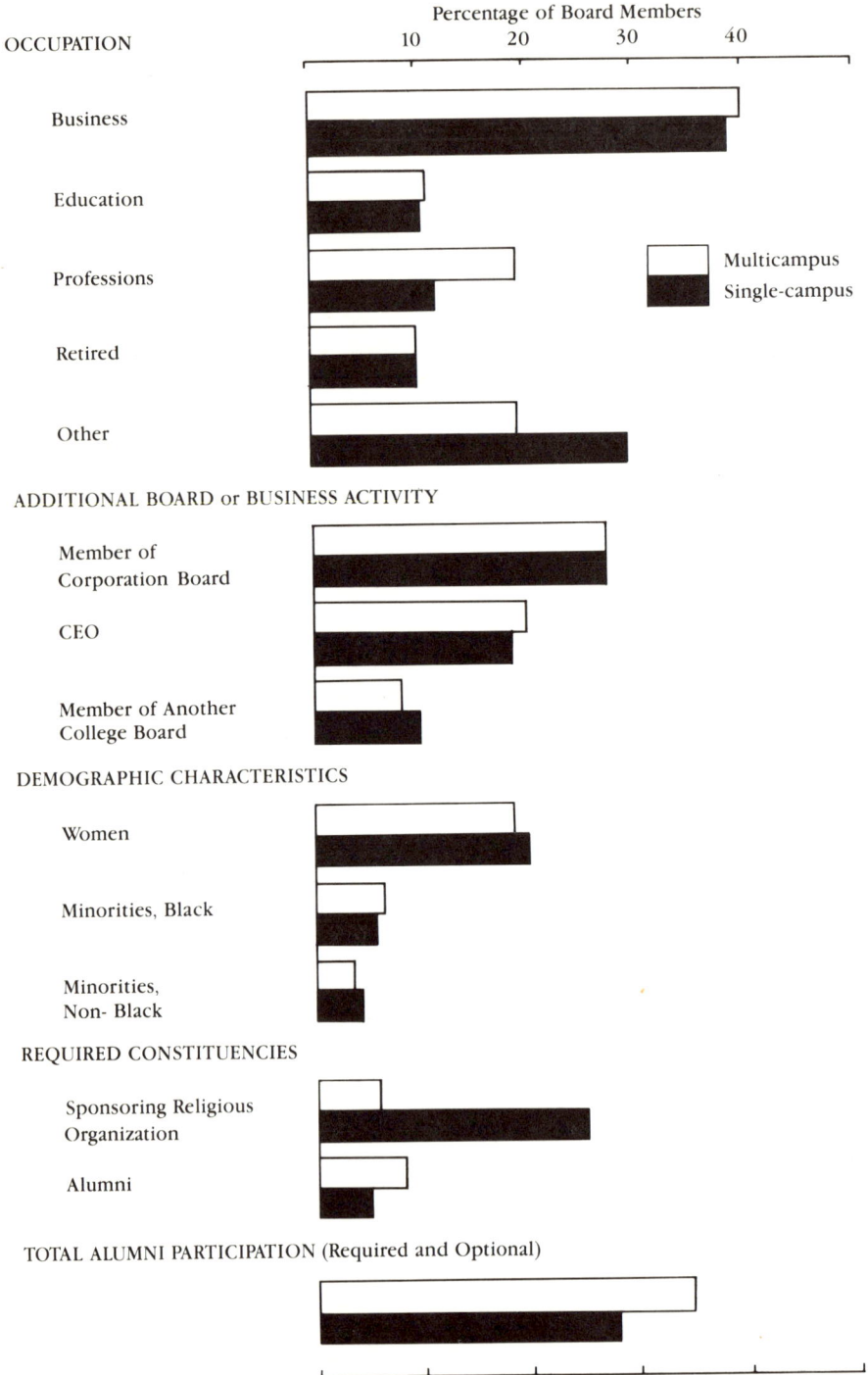

Percentage of Board Members

OCCUPATION

10   20   30   40

Business

Education

Professions

Retired

Other

Multicampus
Single-campus

ADDITIONAL BOARD or BUSINESS ACTIVITY

Member of
Corporation Board

CEO

Member of Another
College Board

DEMOGRAPHIC CHARACTERISTICS

Women

Minorities, Black

Minorities,
Non-Black

REQUIRED CONSTITUENCIES

Sponsoring Religious
Organization

Alumni

TOTAL ALUMNI PARTICIPATION (Required and Optional)

14

Contrasts with 1977 Data

*T*he 1977 survey of governing boards included many of the same general questions as this study. Some questions, however, were less specific or were cast in somewhat different language so that precise comparisons should not be made. The 1977 survey, for example, included foundation executives in the business category. Clergy were included in the professional services classification; retirees were in the "other" category as were accountants and social workers. The 1977 questionnaire asked about membership on boards of other *institutions*. The current survey asks about membership on the board of another *college or university*. The large drop in multiple-board membership (from 19 percent to 10 percent) may be a result of the inclusion of noneducational institutions (hospitals, foundations) in the 1977 results, but it also seems probable that institutions and board members are realizing the amount of time and energy it takes to serve on a board.

The proportion of business people on college and university boards has increased in the eight years since the earlier survey: from 34 percent to 37 percent. On public boards the percentage increased from 31 to 36 percent; on independent boards from 35 to 38 percent. A reduction is shown in the proportion of board members who also sit on corporate boards—from 32 to 27 percent.

The proportion of governing board members who also serve as chairpersons, chief executive officers, or chief operating officers of corporations has dropped half a percentage point (from 18.9 percent to 18.4 percent) since 1977. This coupled with the increased business participation suggests that institutions are now selecting board members from a wider range of executive positions than formerly was the case.

Figure G (see also Table 13 in Appendix A) shows the differences between the two surveys in several selected board member characteristics. Worthy of special attention are the increases in the proportion of women and minorities (other than black), and the stasis in the percentage of blacks. Singled out from the several professions are the lawyers. Notably, their representation on the boards is somewhat smaller than it was eight years ago.

FIGURE G
Selected Characteristics of Board Members 1977 and 1985

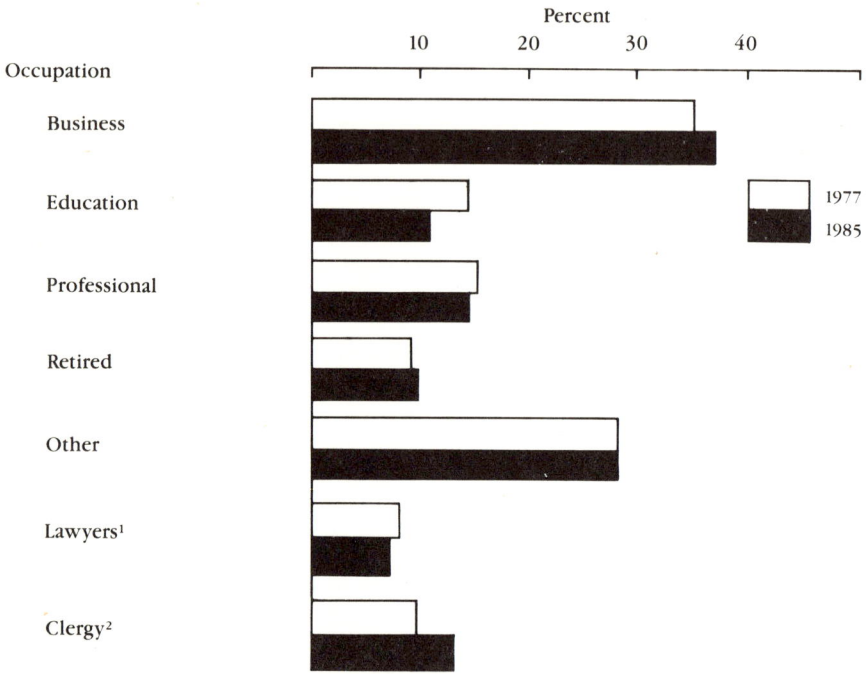

Percent

Occupation

Business

Education   1977
                             1985

Professional

Retired

Other

Lawyers[1]

Clergy[2]

ADDITIONAL BOARD or BUSINESS ACTIVITY

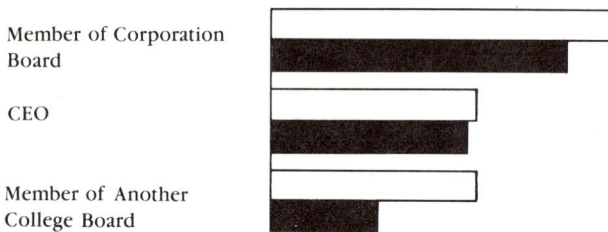

Member of Corporation
Board

CEO

Member of Another
College Board

DEMOGRAPHIC CHARACTERISTICS

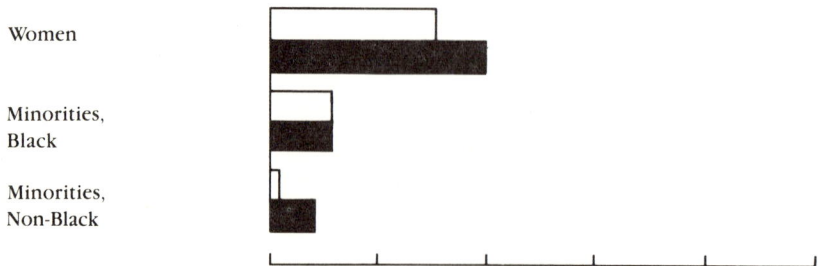

Women

Minorities,
Black

Minorities,
Non-Black

_____
[1] Also included in the "Professional" bar.

[2] Also included in the "Other" bar.

Summary

*T*he characteristics of the boards governing the nation's nonprofit colleges and universities have not changed dramatically since 1977. The total number of boards and active board positions hovers around 2,200 and 48,000 respectively. The count of multicampus boards remains somewhat less than 200, and the campuses that they govern increased by only about 100. This lack of change is not surprising because the last eight years have seen a leveling off of staff and enrollments.

About 20 percent of the governing board members are women. Eight years ago the figure was only 15 percent. The proportion of racial/ethnic minorities remains at less than ten percent, although nonblack minorities have increased slightly.

There is an increase in the representation of business people on governing boards, both public and private, multicampus and single-campus. Nearly half of the board members have linkages with the business community through their current occupation, the position from which they have retired, or their membership on corporate boards. As this participation has increased, the percentage of corporate chairpersons, presidents, or chief executive officers has dropped slightly, implying that institutions are increasingly drawing their board members from a wider executive spectrum of the business world.

Appendix A

Governing Boards and Institutions Governed, by Control

Characteristics	Number of Boards	Number of Institutions Governed	FTE* Enrollment (Fall 1982)**
Total Governing Boards	2,237	3,039	8,841,428
Single-campus	2,050	2,050	4,017,849
Multicampus			
Governing 2–3 institutions	111	268	1,564,878
Governing >3 institutions	76	721	3,258,701
Public	751	1,511	6,811,085
Single-campus	597	597	2,246,967
Multicampus			
Governing 2–3 institutions	79	199	1,322,785
Governing >3 institutions	75	715	3,241,333
Independent	1,486	1,528	2,030,343
Single-campus	1,453	1,453	1,770,882
Multicampus			
Governing 2–3 institutions	32	69	242,093
Governing >3 institutions	1	6	17,368

* Full-time-equivalent enrollment.

** Final 1984 enrollment data were not available at the time the results of the survey were being tabulated. Between 1982 and 1984, national FTE enrollments have changed less than four percent.

TABLE II
Voting Members of Governing Boards

| Voting Members | Total Governing Boards | | | |
| | | | Multicampus | |
	Total N* = 2,237	Single- Campus N = 2,050	≤3** N = 111	>3*** N = 76
Total number authorized	51,663	48,972	1,704	987
Average number authorized	23.1	23.9	15.4	13.0
Total number serving	47,994	45,379	1,646	969
Average number serving	21.5	22.1	14.9	12.7
Proportion serving	92.9	92.7	96.6	98.1
Of number serving, proportion which must come from designated constituencies	42.2	42.4	36.7	41.0
Proportion which must come from sponsoring church organizations	23.6	24.6	10.2	0.0
Proportion which must come from alumni	5.1	4.9	8.4	6.7
Proportion which must come from other	13.5	12.9	18.1	34.3
Proportion of additional board members who are alumni	23.1	23.0	25.3	27.4
Proportion which come from faculty	1.3	1.3	1.7	0.7
Proportion which come from student population	1.2	1.1	2.0	3.7

Note: On this and subsequent tables, independent multicampus governing boards were collapsed into one category because of their small number.

    * N equals the number of boards whose membership is described in the body of the table.

    ** ≤3, Boards governing two or three institutions.

    *** >3, Board governing more than three institutions.

TABLE II (Continued)
Voting Members of Governing Boards

	Public				Independent		
			Multicampus				
	Total N = 751	Single-Campus N = 597	≤ 3 N = 79	> 3 N = 75	Total N = 1,487	Single-Campus N = 1,453	Multi-campus N = 34
	6,528	4,902	670	955	45,135	44,070	1,065
	8.7	8.2	8.5	12.8	30.4	30.3	31.8
	6,481	4,879	665	937	41,513	40,500	1,013
	8.6	8.2	8.5	12.6	27.9	27.9	30.2
	99.3	99.5	99.2	98.1	92.0	91.9	95.1
	43.8	45.2	36.7	41.6	42.0	42.1	36.2
	0.0	0.0	0.0	0.0	27.3	27.6	16.5
	1.6	0.4	4.2	6.2	6.0	5.4	11.6
	42.2	44.8	32.5	35.4	9.1	9.1	8.0
	11.4	6.7	22.4	28.1	25.0	24.9	26.7
	0.2	0.1	0.7	0.7	1.5	1.4	2.4
	1.4	0.9	1.9	3.8	1.1	1.1	2.0

TABLE III
Characteristics of Voting Members of Governing Boards
(In Percentages)

Characteristics	Total N* = 2,237	Single-Campus N = 2,050	Multicampus ≤3** N = 79	Multicampus >3*** N = 76
Total number serving	47,994	45,379	1,646	969
Sex:				
Men	79.9	79.8	82.9	80.7
Women	20.1	20.2	17.1	19.3
Total	100.0	100.0	100.0	100.0
Race:				
White	90.1	90.1	91.6	87.6
Black	6.3	6.2	6.0	9.1
Hispanic	0.6	0.6	2.2	1.5
Other	3.0	3.1	0.2	1.8
Total	100.0	100.0	100.0	100.0
Education:				
Less than high school	.0	.0	0.1	0.1
High school diploma	4.4	4.3	5.9	6.5
Associate's degree	2.9	3.0	2.5	3.1
Bachelor's degree	40.2	40.2	41.7	40.3
Master's degree	22.8	23.1	18.5	15.7
Professional degree	18.9	18.7	21.7	24.8
Doctoral degree	10.7	10.7	9.5	9.5
Total	100.0	100.0	99.9	100.0
Age:				
Less than 30 years old	2.0	2.0	2.2	3.6
30–39 years old	6.8	6.7	7.7	8.2
40–49 years old	20.8	20.7	21.6	24.5
50–59 years old	38.1	38.2	37.5	34.9
60–69 years old	24.1	24.2	22.6	23.5
70 years old or older	8.2	8.2	8.4	5.4
Total	100.0	100.0	100.0	100.0

* N equals the number of boards whose membership is described in the body of the tables.

** ≤3, Boards governing two or three institutions.

*** >3, Boards governing more than three institutions.

TABLE III (Continued)
Characteristics of Voting Members of Governing Boards
(In Percentages)

Public				Independent		
Total Public N = 751	Single-Campus N = 597	Multicampus ≤3 N = 79	Multicampus >3 N = 75	Total Indep't. N = 1,487	Single-Campus N = 1,453	Multi-campus N = 34
6,481	4,879	665	937	41,513	40,500	1,013
76.9	75.9	78.7	80.9	80.4	80.3	85.5
23.1	24.1	21.3	19.1	19.6	19.7	14.5
100.0	100.0	100.0	100.0	100.0	100.0	100.0
85.2	84.8	84.9	87.5	90.9	90.8	96.0
11.4	12.0	10.3	9.1	5.5	5.5	3.2
2.7	2.7	4.5	1.6	0.3	0.3	0.7
0.7	0.5	0.3	1.8	3.3	3.4	0.1
100.0	100.0	100.0	100.0	100.0	100.0	100.0
0.0	0.0	0.2	0.1	0.0	0.0	0.0
9.1	9.9	7.3	6.6	3.7	3.6	4.9
5.0	5.5	3.7	3.2	2.6	2.7	1.6
38.8	38.7	38.3	40.0	40.5	40.4	44.1
18.2	18.5	20.4	15.3	23.5	23.6	17.6
21.8	20.9	23.1	25.5	18.5	18.4	20.2
6.9	6.5	6.5	9.3	11.2	11.2	11.6
99.8	100.0	99.7	100.0	100.0	100.0	100.0
1.8	1.4	2.2	3.7	2.1	2.1	2.1
10.8	11.2	11.3	8.3	6.2	6.2	5.3
26.4	26.7	26.7	24.6	19.9	20.0	18.3
32.8	32.2	34.3	35.1	38.9	38.9	39.2
22.7	23.2	19.1	22.9	24.3	24.3	25.5
5.5	5.4	6.4	5.4	8.6	8.6	9.5
100.0	100.0	100.0	100.0	100.0	100.0	100.0

TABLE IV
Primary Occupations of Voting Members of Governing Boards
(In Percentages)

Primary Occupation	Total Governing Boards			
			Multicampus	
	Total N* = 2,237	Single-Campus N = 2,050	≤3** N = 111	>3*** N = 76
Total number serving	47,994	45,379	1,646	969
Business:				
Executive, large corp.	13.5	13.4	15.5	14.5
Executive, banking firm	10.2	10.0	15.8	10.4
Executive, small business	12.4	12.6	8.9	11.1
Entrepreneur	0.5	0.5	0.9	0.6
Executive	0.3	0.3	0.9	0.5
Other	0.6	0.7	0.2	0.0
Education:				
Officer, higher education	3.2	3.2	3.2	2.4
Faculty, higher education	2.9	3.0	2.6	1.7
Full-time student	0.9	0.8	2.2	3.6
Teacher/administrator, primary or secondary school	3.4	3.5	3.5	2.3
Elementary/Secondary System administrator	0.3	0.3	0.2	0.6
Higher education administrator	0.0	0.0	0.0	0.1
Other	0.2	0.2	0.4	0.4
Professional Service:				
Accountant	0.9	0.9	0.6	1.3
Dentist	0.7	0.7	0.9	1.0
Lawyer	6.5	6.2	9.8	14.6
Physician	3.1	3.1	3.0	2.6
Psychologist	0.2	0.2	0.4	0.2
Social Worker	0.4	0.4	0.4	0.6
Consultant	0.2	0.2	0.8	0.2
Scientist, Engineer	0.7	0.7	0.4	0.2
Allied Health	0.4	0.4	0.4	1.0
Architect	0.1	0.1	0.2	0.2
Other	0.4	0.4	0.1	0.2
Retired:				
Corporate/Financial Officer	4.4	4.4	4.6	3.0
Educator	1.7	1.7	1.9	3.4
Professional	2.2	2.2	0.9	1.5
Other	1.3	1.3	2.0	1.6

* N equals the number of boards whose membership is described in the body of the table.
** ≤3, Boards governing two or three institutions.
*** >3, Board governing more than three institutions.

TABLE IV (Continued)
Primary Occupations of Voting Members of Governing Boards
(In Percentages)

	Public			Independent		
Total Public N = 751	Single-Campus N = 597	Multicampus ≤3 N = 79	Multicampus >3 N = 75	Total Indep't. N = 1,487	Single-Campus N = 1,453	Multi-campus N = 34
6,481	4,879	665	937	41,513	40,500	1,013
10.5	9.9	10.7	13.9	13.9	13.8	19.2
9.0	8.3	12.4	10.2	10.4	10.2	18.0
14.8	15.9	11.5	11.5	12.0	12.2	6.9
0.7	0.5	1.7	0.6	0.5	0.5	0.4
0.6	0.6	0.7	0.5	0.2	0.2	1.0
0.7	0.9	0.5	0.0	0.6	0.6	0.0
1.3	1.1	1.2	2.3	3.5	3.4	4.5
0.9	0.7	1.2	1.7	3.3	3.3	3.4
1.1	0.5	1.9	3.7	0.9	0.9	2.3
5.9	6.5	6.0	2.3	3.1	3.1	1.7
0.4	0.4	0.2	0.6	0.3	0.3	0.1
0.0	0.0	0.0	0.1	0.0	0.0	0.0
0.3	0.3	0.5	0.4	0.2	0.1	0.3
1.0	1.0	0.5	1.2	0.9	0.9	0.8
2.0	2.2	1.4	1.0	0.5	0.5	0.6
10.4	9.3	11.6	15.0	5.9	5.8	8.5
4.9	5.5	3.1	2.7	2.8	2.8	2.9
0.1	0.1	0.0	0.2	0.2	0.2	0.7
1.2	1.4	0.5	0.6	0.3	0.3	0.3
0.2	0.1	0.7	0.2	0.2	0.2	0.9
0.9	0.9	1.0	0.2	0.6	0.7	0.0
1.6	1.8	0.7	0.9	0.2	0.2	0.4
0.1	0.0	0.0	0.2	0.1	0.1	0.2
0.6	0.7	0.2	0.2	0.4	0.4	0.0
2.7	2.6	2.9	2.8	4.7	4.6	5.8
5.3	5.8	3.9	3.6	1.2	1.2	0.6
2.1	2.4	1.0	1.6	2.2	2.2	0.9
1.8	1.7	2.2	1.7	1.2	1.2	1.8

Table IV continued on next page.

TABLE IV (Continued)
Primary Occupations of Voting Members of Governing Boards
(In Percentages)

Primary Occupation	Total N* = 2,237	Single-Campus N = 2,050	Multicampus ≤3** N = 111	Multicampus >3*** N = 76
Other:				
Administrative officer/executive, nonprofit organization	3.6	3.8	1.7	1.9
Artist/writer/musician	0.6	0.6	0.2	0.0
Clergy	12.5	13.0	4.2	1.2
Govt. official, elected	1.2	1.1	1.5	3.0
Govt. official, non-elected	1.1	1.0	1.7	2.3
Farmer/rancher	1.2	1.1	2.0	3.8
Homemaker	4.9	5.0	3.3	3.9
Journalist	0.6	0.6	0.5	0.6
Judge	0.6	0.6	1.2	0.5
Labor official	0.1	0.1	0.8	1.8
Skilled/semi-skilled worker	0.4	0.4	0.2	0.1
Civic worker/volunteer	0.7	0.7	0.6	0.1
Military	0.0	0.0	0.1	0.0
Other	0.7	0.7	0.8	0.7
Total	99.9	100.0	99.5	100.0

* N equals the number of boards whose membership is described in the body of the table.

** ≤3, Boards governing two or three institutions.

*** >3, Board governing more than three institutions.

TABLE V
Additional Activities of Voting Members of Governing Boards
(In Percentages)

Activity	Total N* = 2,237	Single-Campus N = 2,050	Multicampus ≤3** N = 111	Multicampus >3*** N = 76
Total number serving	47,994	45,379	1,646	969
Proportion who are members of another governing board	9.6	9.7	8.9	7.5
Proportion who are members of a corporation board	26.6	26.6	28.4	25.5
Proportion who are president or chairman of a corporation	18.4	18.3	20.6	18.9

* N equals the number of boards whose membership is described in the body of the table.

** ≤3, Boards governing two or three institutions.

*** >3, Board governing more than three institutions.

TABLE IV (Continued)
Primary Occupations of Voting Members of Governing Boards
(In Percentages)

	Public			Independent		
Total Public N = 751	Single-Campus N = 597	Multicampus ≤3 N = 79	Multicampus >3 N = 75	Total Indep't. N = 1,487	Single-Campus N = 1,453	Multi-campus N = 34
1.5	1.4	1.9	1.7	4.0	4.0	1.8
0.2	0.2	0.0	0.0	0.6	0.6	0.3
1.0	0.9	0.9	1.2	14.3	14.5	6.3
1.3	0.9	1.7	3.1	1.1	1.1	1.3
2.0	1.8	3.1	2.3	1.0	1.0	0.8
4.4	4.5	4.1	3.8	0.7	0.7	0.7
5.8	6.2	5.5	4.1	4.8	4.9	1.8
0.6	0.6	0.7	0.5	0.6	0.6	0.5
0.4	0.5	0.3	0.5	0.6	0.6	1.7
0.5	0.2	1.2	1.8	0.1	0.1	0.5
0.6	0.7	0.5	0.1	0.4	0.4	0.0
0.2	0.3	0.5	0.0	0.7	0.7	0.8
0.2	0.2	0.2	0.0	0.0	0.0	0.0
0.5	0.4	1.0	0.7	0.8	0.8	0.7
99.8	99.7	99.8	100.0	100.0	100.0	99.4

TABLE V (Continued)
Additional Activities of Voting Members of Governing Boards
(In Percentages)

	Public			Independent		
Total Public N = 751	Single-Campus N = 597	Multicampus ≤3 N = 79	Multicampus >3 N = 75	Total Indep't. N = 1,487	Single-Campus N = 1,453	Multi-campus N = 34
6,481	4,879	665	937	41,513	40,500	1,013
4.2	3.7	4.2	7.1	10.4	10.4	12.3
14.5	11.3	22.6	25.1	28.5	28.4	32.4
11.3	9.4	15.4	18.6	19.5	19.4	24.2

TABLE VI
Selected Characteristics of Single-Campus Governing Boards
(In Percentages)

Characteristic	Total N* = 2,050	Public N = 597	Independent N = 1,453
Total	100.0	29.1	70.9
Type:			
University	2.7	2.0	3.0
Four-year College	58.6	18.8	75.0
Two-year College	38.7	79.2	22.0
Census Region:			
East	19.5	8.77	23.9
Midwest	31.4	23.5	34.6
South	34.9	43.9	31.1
West	14.3	23.7	10.4
FTE Enrollment:			
600 or fewer	38.7	13.3	49.1
601–1,500	26.6	20.3	29.2
1,501–5,000	23.9	39.6	17.4
5,001–10,000	7.7	18.5	3.2
More than 10,000	3.1	8.11	1.0

* N equals the number of boards whose membership is described in the body of the table.

TABLE VII
Voting Members of Single-Campus Governing Boards
(In Percentages)

Voting Members	Public Single-Campus Boards			Independent Single-Campus Boards		
	University N* = 12	Four-Year N = 112	Two-Year N = 473	University N = 43	Four-Year N = 1,090	Two-Year N = 320
Total number authorized	192	1,033	3,676	1,747	32,695	9,684
Average number authorized	16.4	9.2	7.8	40.3	30.0	30.3
Total number serving	192	1,017	3,670	1,693	29,966	8,840
Average number serving	16.4	9.1	7.8	39.1	27.5	27.6
Proportion serving	100.0	98.4	99.8	97.0	91.7	91.3
Of number serving, Proportion which must come from designated constituencies	28.0	31.3	49.9	11.9	44.8	38.8
Proportion which must come from sponsoring church organizations	0.0	0.0	0.0	3.5	30.8	21.4
Proportion which must come from alumni	8.8	0.3	0.0	8.2	6.4	1.6
Proportion which must come from other	19.1	31.0	49.9	0.3	7.6	15.8
Proportion of additional board members who are alumni	35.8	11.8	3.8	40.4	27.1	14.8
Proportion which come from faculty	0.0	0.3	0.0	0.7	1.7	0.7
Proportion which come from student population	2.9	2.0	0.5	0.3	1.1	1.3

* N equals the number of boards whose membership is described in the body of the table.

TABLE VIII
Characteristics of Voting Members of Single-Campus Governing Boards
(In Percentages)

Characteristics	Public Single-Campus Boards			Independent Single-Campus Boards		
	University N* = 12	Four-Year N = 112	Two-Year N = 473	University N = 43	Four-Year N = 1,090	Two-Year N = 320
Number of voting members	192	1,017	3,670	1,693	29,966	8,840
Sex:						
Men	86.8	76.3	75.2	88.0	80.3	78.6
Women	13.2	23.7	24.8	12.0	19.7	21.4
Total	100.0	100.0	100.0	100.0	100.0	100.0
Race:						
White	82.1	68.9	89.4	92.2	93.0	82.9
Black	17.9	27.5	7.4	6.7	5.0	6.9
Hispanic	0.0	3.6	2.6	0.7	0.4	0.0
Other	0.0	0.0	0.6	0.4	1.6	10.2
Total	100.0	100.0	100.0	100.0	100.0	100.0
Education:						
Less than high school	0.0	0.0	0.0	0.0	0.1	0.0
High school diploma	7.4	8.1	10.5	3.3	3.3	4.9
Associate's degree	0.0	0.0	7.3	0.9	1.8	5.9
Bachelor's degree	37.1	28.3	41.7	37.5	39.3	44.7
Master's degree	20.5	20.4	17.9	16.7	25.0	20.4
Professional degree	31.8	29.4	18.0	27.2	19.1	14.5
Doctoral degree	3.2	13.8	4.7	14.3	11.6	9.5
Total	100.0	100.0	100.0	100.0	100.0	100.0
Age:						
Less than 30 years old	2.9	2.6	0.9	1.3	1.7	3.6
30–39 years old	6.1	13.0	10.9	3.2	6.1	6.9
40–49 years old	18.5	25.0	27.6	15.8	20.6	18.8
50–59 years old	37.9	30.5	32.3	35.5	41.1	32.2
60–69 years old	25.5	22.7	23.2	33.7	23.9	24.0
70 years old or older	9.1	6.1	4.9	10.5	6.7	14.5
Total	100.0	100.0	100.0	100.0	100.0	100.0

* N equals the number of boards whose membership is described in the body of the table.

TABLE IX
Primary Occupations of Voting Members of Single-Campus Governing Boards
(In Percentages)

Primary Occupation	Public Single-Campus Boards			Independent Single-Campus Boards		
	University N* = 12	Four-Year N = 112	Two-Year N = 473	University N = 43	Four-Year N = 1,090	Two-Year N = 320
Number of voting members	192	1,017	3,670	1,693	29,966	8,840
Business:						
Executive, large corp.	22.1	10.1	9.2	24.3	14.8	8.2
Executive, banking firm	7.8	9.6	7.9	20.3	10.4	7.6
Executive, small business	7.4	10.7	17.8	10.7	10.5	18.1
Entrepreneur	1.5	0.3	0.5	0.1	0.6	0.3
Executive	1.5	0.3	0.6	0.1	0.3	0.0
Other	0.0	0.0	1.2	0.3	0.6	1.0
Education:						
Officer, higher education	1.5	2.3	0.7	6.2	3.1	3.9
Faculty, higher education	1.5	0.3	0.7	1.6	3.6	2.3
Full-time student	2.9	1.3	0.1	0.6	1.0	0.7
Teacher/administrator, primary or secondary school	2.9	7.5	6.5	0.6	2.4	5.9
Elementary/Secondary System administrator	1.5	0.3	0.3	0.1	0.1	0.7
Higher education administrator	0.0	0.0	0.0	0.1	0.0	0.0
Other	0.0	0.0	0.3	0.1	0.2	0.0
Professional Service:						
Accountant	0.0	0.7	1.2	1.0	0.9	1.0
Dentist	1.5	1.6	2.4	0.9	0.5	0.3
Lawyer	12.0	14.6	7.7	9.2	6.3	3.6
Physician	4.9	8.6	4.7	2.2	3.1	2.0
Psychologist	0.0	0.7	0.0	0.0	0.1	0.3
Social Worker	0.0	1.6	1.4	0.0	0.3	0.3
Consultant	0.0	0.0	0.1	0.9	0.2	0.3
Scientist, Engineer	0.0	0.0	1.3	0.4	0.7	0.7
Allied Health	0.0	0.6	2.2	0.1	0.1	0.7
Architect	1.7	0.0	0.3	0.1	0.1	0.0
Other	0.0	0.3	0.8	0.0	0.4	0.7
Retired:						
Corporate/Financial Officer	4.4	1.5	2.9	6.6	3.7	7.6
Educator	1.5	7.9	5.4	0.3	0.9	2.3
Professional	0.0	2.0	2.6	0.3	1.8	3.9
Other	1.5	1.9	1.6	1.2	1.4	0.7

* N equals the number of boards whose membership is described in the body of the table.

Table IX continued on next page.

TABLE IX (Continued)
Primary Occupations of Voting Members of Single-Campus Governing Boards (In Percentages)

Primary Occupation	Public Single-Campus Boards			Independent Single-Campus Boards		
	University N* = 12	Four-Year N = 112	Two-Year N = 473	University N = 43	Four-Year N = 1,090	Two-Year N = 320
Other:						
Administrative officer/ executive, nonprofit organization	0.0	3.3	0.9	2.8	4.2	3.6
Artist/writer/musician	1.5	0.0	0.2	0.4	0.4	1.3
Clergy	1.5	1.3	0.8	3.3	16.5	9.9
Govt. official, elected	5.9	2.6	0.2	0.9	0.7	2.6
Govt. official, nonelected	1.5	1.3	2.0	0.6	0.9	1.3
Farmer/rancher	0.0	2.0	5.4	0.3	0.5	1.3
Homemaker	1.5	2.4	7.4	1.0	5.8	2.6
Journalist	0.0	1.0	0.5	0.1	0.7	0.3
Judge	5.9	0.6	0.1	1.0	0.5	0.7
Labor official	0.0	0.0	0.2	0.0	0.1	0.0
Skilled/semi-skilled worker	0.0	0.0	0.9	0.0	0.5	0.3
Civic worker/volunteer	4.4	0.0	0.1	0.7	0.5	1.3
Military	0.0	0.0	0.3	0.0	0.0	0.0
Other	0.0	0.6	0.3	0.3	0.6	1.6
Total	100.0	100.0	100.0	100.0	100.0	100.0

* N equals the number of boards whose membership is described in the body of the table.

TABLE X
Additional Activities of Voting Members of Single-Campus Governing Boards (In Percentages)

Primary Occupation	Public Single-Campus Boards			Independent Single-Campus Boards		
	University N* = 12	Four-Year N = 112	Two-Year N = 473	University N = 43	Four-Year N = 1,090	Two-Year N = 320
Number of voting members	192	1,017	3,670	1,693	29,966	8,840
Proportion who are members of another governing board	9.5	4.2	3.3	17.0	10.8	7.9
Proportion who are members of a corporation board	28.0	12.2	10.2	57.8	24.4	36.5
Proportion who are president or chairman of a corporation	12.4	5.9	10.2	44.7	18.3	18.1

* N equals the number of boards whose membership is described in the body of the table.

TABLE XI
Change in Distribution of Governing Boards and Institutions Governed, by Control

Characteristic	Boards		Institutions	
	1977	1985	1977	1985
Total Governing Boards	100.0	100.0	100.0	100.0
Single-campus	92.9	91.6	70.8	70.6
Multicampus				
Governing 2–3 institutions	4.0	5.0	7.3	7.8
Governing >3 institutions	3.1	3.4	21.9	21.6
Public				
Single-campus	27.3	26.7	20.8	20.6
Multicampus				
Governing 2–3 institutions	3.1	3.5	5.8	6.0
Governing >3 institutions	2.9	3.4	21.1	21.5
Independent				
Single-campus	65.6	64.9	50.0	50.1
Multicampus				
Governing 2–3 institutions	0.9	1.4	1.5	1.7
Governing >3 institutions	0.2	0.1	0.8	0.1

TABLE XII
Change in Number of Board Members and Size of Boards

	Total Governing Boards		
	Total	Single-Campus	Multi-campus
Total Number Authorized			
1977	50,537	48,071	2,466
1985	51,663	48,972	2,691
Average Number Authorized			
1977	21.8	22.4	15.0
1985	23.1	23.9	14.4
Total Number Serving			
1977	47,138	44,759	2,379
1985	47,994	45,379	2,615
Average Number Serving			
1977	20.4	20.8	14.5
1985	21.5	22.1	14.0
Proportion Serving			
1977	93.3	93.1	96.5
1985	92.9	92.7	97.2

TABLE XII (Continued)
Change in Number of Board Members and Size of Boards

Public			Independent		
Total	Single-Campus	Multi-campus	Total	Single-Campus	Multi-campus
7,044	5,560	1,484	43,493	42,511	982
6,528	4,902	1,626	45,135	44,070	1,065
9.1	8.8	10.8	28.2	28.0	37.8
8.7	8.2	10.6	30.4	30.3	31.8
6,913	5,458	1,455	40,225	39,301	924
6,481	4,879	1,602	41,513	40,500	1,013
9.0	8.6	10.5	26.1	25.9	35.5
8.6	8.2	10.5	27.9	27.9	30.2
98.1	98.2	98.0	92.5	92.4	94.1
99.3	99.5	98.5	92.0	91.9	95.1

TABLE XIII
Change in Characteristics of Governing Board Members

	Total Governing Boards					
	Total		Single-Campus		Multi-campus	
	1977	1985	1977	1985	1977	1985
Percent Who Are						
Sex:						
Men	84.9	79.9	84.9	79.8	85.5	82.1
Women	15.1	20.1	15.1	20.2	14.7	17.9
Total	100.0	100.0	100.0	100.0	100.0	100.0
Race:						
White	93.0	90.1	93.1	90.1	92.0	90.1
Black	6.0	6.3	5.9	6.2	6.3	7.1
Hispanic	*NA	0.6	NA	0.6	NA	2.0
Other minority	1.0	3.0	1.0	3.1	1.7	0.8
Total	100.0	100.0	100.0	100.0	100.0	100.0
Education:						
Less than high school	0.4	0.0	0.3	0.0	2.0	0.1
High school diploma	6.5	4.4	6.5	4.3	7.0	6.1
AA, AS	2.8	2.9	2.8	3.0	2.4	2.7
BA, BS	38.8	40.2	38.8	40.2	38.4	41.2
MA, MS, MAT	19.4	22.8	19.6	23.1	15.6	17.5
MD, JD	21.2	18.9	21.0	18.7	25.3	22.8
Ph.D, Ed.D	11.0	10.7	11.1	10.7	9.3	9.5
Total	100.0	100.0	100.0	100.0	100.0	99.9
Age:						
Less than 30 years	2.2	2.0	2.1	2.0	3.6	2.7
30–39 years	7.3	6.8	7.3	6.7	6.2	7.9
40–49 years	24.4	20.8	24.3	20.7	24.8	22.7
50–59 years	35.0	38.1	34.9	38.2	37.0	36.5
60–69 years	24.7	24.1	24.8	24.2	23.2	22.9
70 years and older	6.5	8.2	6.6	8.2	5.1	7.2
Total	100.0	100.0	100.0	100.0	100.0	100.0

* Not Available

TABLE XIII (Continued)
Change in Characteristics of Governing Board Members

Public						Independent					
Public Total		Single-Campus		Multi-campus		Independent Total		Single-Campus		Multi-campus	
1977	1985	1977	1985	1977	1985	1977	1985	1977	1985	1977	1985
82.3	76.9	81.7	75.9	84.4	80.0	85.3	80.4	85.3	80.3	87.3	85.5
17.7	23.1	18.3	24.1	15.6	20.0	14.7	19.6	14.7	19.7	12.7	14.5
100.0	100.0	100.0	100.0	100.0	100.0	100.0	100.0	100.0	100.0	100.0	100.0
92.9	85.2	94.0	84.8	88.9	86.4	94.1	90.9	94.0	90.8	96.8	96.0
5.9	11.4	5.2	12.0	8.4	9.6	5.1	5.5	5.2	5.5	2.9	3.2
NA	2.7	NA	2.7	NA	2.8	NA	0.3	NA	0.3	NA	0.7
1.1	0.7	0.7	0.5	2.6	1.2	0.7	3.3	0.7	3.4	0.3	0.0
100.0	100.0	100.0	100.0	100.0	100.0	100.0	100.0	100.0	100.0	100.0	99.9
1.2	.0	0.7	0.0	3.3	0.1	0.3	.0	0.3	.0	0	0.0
10.9	9.1	11.8	9.9	7.6	6.9	5.8	3.7	5.8	3.6	5.9	4.9
4.5	5.0	4.8	5.5	3.6	3.4	2.5	2.6	2.5	2.7	0.7	1.6
37.8	38.8	37.7	38.7	38.3	39.3	38.9	40.5	38.9	40.4	38.4	44.1
17.1	18.2	17.5	18.5	15.4	17.4	19.7	23.5	19.8	23.6	16.0	17.6
22.5	21.8	21.6	20.9	25.8	24.5	21.0	18.5	20.9	18.4	24.3	20.2
5.9	6.9	5.9	6.5	6.1	8.2	11.9	11.2	11.8	11.2	14.6	11.6
100.0	100.0	100.0	100.0	100.0	99.9	100.0	100.0	100.0	100.0	100.0	100.0
2.7	1.8	2.2	1.4	4.5	3.1	2.1	2.1	2.1	2.1	2.3	2.1
9.3	10.8	9.6	11.2	8.3	9.6	6.9	6.2	7.0	6.2	3.0	5.3
31.5	26.4	32.9	26.7	26.3	25.5	23.2	19.9	23.2	20.0	22.4	18.3
34.4	32.8	33.7	32.2	37.0	34.8	35.0	38.9	35.0	38.9	37.1	39.2
17.3	22.7	16.9	23.2	18.6	21.3	25.9	24.3	25.8	24.3	30.5	25.5
4.6	5.5	4.6	5.4	4.8	5.8	6.8	8.6	6.8	8.6	4.7	9.5
100.0	100.0	100.0	100.0	100.0	100.0	100.0	100.0	100.0	100.0	100.0	100.0

TABLE XIV
Additional Activities of Members of Governing Boards
1977 and 1985

| | Total Governing Boards | | | | | |
| | Total | | Single-Campus | | Multi-campus | |
	1977	1985	1977	1985	1977	1985
Percent Who Are:						
Members of another Governing Board	18.8	9.6	18.8	9.7	18.10	8.4
Members of a Corporate Board	31.5	26.6	31.5	26.6	32.92	27.3
President or Chairman of a Corporation	18.9	18.4	18.9	18.3	18.77	19.9

TABLE XIV (Continued)
Additional Activities of Members of Governing Boards
1977 and 1985

Public						Independent					
Total		Single-Campus		Multi-campus		Total		Single-Campus		Multi-campus	
1977	1985	1977	1985	1977	1985	1977	1985	1977	1985	1977	1985
7.9	4.2	7.0	3.7	11.3	5.9	20.6	10.4	20.4	10.4	28.9	12.3
24.1	14.5	23.1	11.3	27.9	24.1	32.8	28.5	32.6	28.4	40.8	32.4
12.0	11.4	11.2	9.4	14.8	17.3	20.1	19.5	20.0	19.4	25.0	24.2

Appendix B

American Council on Education
Higher Education Panel Survey No. 70

Composition of College and University Governing Boards, 1985

1. Please check below the type of governing board that serves your institution:

   ☐ **Single-campus governing board:**
   Legal responsibility for the direct control and operation of a single campus or institutional unit.

   ☐ **Multicampus (or system) governing board:**
   Legal responsibility for the direct control and operation of two or more separately administered campuses, each of which is headed by its own chief executive officer.

   The board is the state-wide and/or system governing board. _____ Yes _____ No

2. How many **voting** members are **authorized** for the board? _____

3. How many **voting** members are now **actually serving** on the board? _____

> The remainder of this survey pertains only to the **voting** members **actually serving** on the board, as reported in Item 3 above.

4. How many board members **must** come from the following designated constituencies?

   a. Sponsoring church organizations? _____

   b. Alumni/alumnae? _____

   c. Other? Please specify.

   _____ _____

5. How many additional board members are alumni/alumnae? _____

6. How many board members come from your institution's faculty? _____

7. How many board members come from your institution's student population? _____

> **Please note:** The total number of board members reported in each of items 8a–e should be the same as the total reported in Item 3 above.

8. Please describe the voting board members according to the following.

   a. **Age** (estimate if necessary)
   How many are:

   _____ Under 30 years old   _____ 50–59 years old

   _____ 30–39 years old   _____ 60–69 years old

   _____ 40–49 years old   _____ 70 years old or older

   b. **Sex**
   How many are:

   _____ Men   _____ Women

   c. **Race**
   How many are:

   _____ White   _____ Hispanic

   _____ Black   _____ Other minority

   d. **Highest Level of Formal Education**
   How many have:

   _____ Less than high school diploma

   _____ High school diploma/equivalency

   _____ Associate's degree
   (A.A., A.S.)

   _____ Bachelor's degree
   (B.A., B.S.)

   _____ Master's degree
   (M.A., M.S., M.A.T.)

   _____ Professional degree
   (M.D., D.D.S., D.V.M., J.D., LL.B.)

   _____ Doctoral degree
   (Ph.D., Sc.D.)

CONTINUED ON NEXT PAGE

| Please review the entire list of possible occupations on this page before filling out this section. |

e. **Primary Occupation**
How many board members are involved in each of the following as a primary vocation? Please count each board member only **once.**

Business

_____ An executive of a large business corporation

_____ An executive of a banking, financial, insurance, or real estate company

_____ An executive of a smaller business

_____ Other (please specify) _____

Education

_____ Officer/administrator of an institution of higher education

_____ Faculty member of an institution of higher education

_____ Full-time student

_____ Teacher/administrator of a primary/secondary school

_____ Other (specify) _____

Professional Service

_____ Accountant

_____ Dentist

_____ Lawyer/partner in a law firm

_____ Physician

_____ Psychologist

_____ Social Worker

_____ Other (specify) _____

Retired

_____ Corporate or financial officer

_____ Educator

_____ Professional

_____ Other (specify) _____

Other

_____ Administrative officer/executive of a nonprofit foundation/organization

_____ Artist/writer/musician

_____ Clergy

_____ Government official, elected

_____ Government official, non-elected

_____ Farmer/rancher

_____ Homemaker

_____ Journalist

_____ Judge

_____ Labor official

_____ Skilled or semi-skilled worker

_____ Other (specify) _____

9. How many board members **also** serve in any of the following capacities?

_____ A member of another governing board of a college or university?

_____ A member of a board of a corporation?

_____ The chairman, chief executive officer, or chief operating officer of a corporation?

Thank you for your assistance. Please return this form by **May 6, 1985,** to:

Higher Education Panel
American Council on Education
One Dupont Circle, Suite 829
Washington, D.C. 20036-1193

Please retain a copy of this survey for your records.

Person completing form:

Name _____

Title _____

Telephone (_____) _____

If you have any questions, please call the HEP staff collect at (202) 833-4757.

Appendix C

Highlights from the 1977 Survey

Board Profile

- More than 47,000 trustees and regents serve on 2,314 governing boards responsible for 3,036 colleges and universities. Approximately 85 percent of these board members are in the private sector of higher education.
- One hundred and sixty-four multicampus boards govern 866 institutions enrolling more than one-half of all students (full-time equivalent).
- About 3,400 trustee positions on governing boards stand vacant at any given time, with almost all of these vacancies existing in the private sector.
- Boards governing private institutions average 26 trustees, whereas boards governing public institutions average nine trustees.
- Nationally, 3 of 10 trustees must be selected from designated constituencies or special groups, with as many as six percent selected from alumni.

Trustee Profile

- Fifteen percent of all trustees are women and 18 percent of the trustees of public single-campus boards are women.
- Seven percent of all trustees are members of minority groups; the proportion averages as high as 14 percent on public single-campus institutions and as low as three percent on private multicampus boards.
- Ninety percent of all trustees have at least a baccalaureate, and 32 percent have a professional or doctoral degree.
- Two of three trustees are age 50 or older, and only 1 in 10 is under age 40. Younger trustees tend to be on the boards of public institutions.
- Thirty-four percent of all trustees are executives or administrators in business and industry, not including those who have retired from this occupational group.
- Nineteen percent of all trustees are presidents of corporations or board chairpersons; 32 percent of all trustees are members of at least one corporate board.
- Nearly 25 percent of all trustees are lawyers, doctors, or members of the clergy.
- Overall, 13 percent of trustees are employed in education, as teachers or administrators; another one percent are college students.
- Nineteen percent hold trusteeships on more than one governing board.